A Z O R E S

poems

AZORES

DAVID YEZZI

Swallow Press / Ohio University Press
Athens

Swallow Press / Ohio University Press, Athens, Ohio 45701
www.ohioswallow.com

© 2008 by David Yezzi

Swallow Press / Ohio University Press books are
printed on acid-free paper ∞ ™

16 15 14 13 12 11 10 09 08   5 4 3 2 1

Library of Congress Cataloging-in-Publication Data

Yezzi, David.
  Azores : poems / David Yezzi.
    p. cm.
  ISBN 978-0-8040-1112-9 (cloth : alk. paper) —
ISBN 978-0-8040-1113-6 (pbk.. : alk. paper)
  I. Title.

PS3625.E99A96 2008
811'.6—dc22

2007047619

Acknowledgments

The Atlantic Monthly	"Acceptance Speech"
Cimarron Review	"The True Mirror"
The Cortland Review	"In the Morning"
Harvard Divinity Bulletin	"Befana, A Bedtime Story," "Vigil"
Image	"The People"
New England Review	"The Call," "Lenten Retreat"
The New York Sun	"Scaffolds"
Parnassus: Poetry in Review	"333 East 68th Street," "Dead Letters," "The Visitor"
Pequod	"A Brief Scene"
Poetry	"Mother Carey's Hen," "The Good News," "Tritina for Susannah"
Southwest Review	"Very Like a Whale"
The Yale Review	"Azores"

"The Call" was reprinted in *The Best American Poetry* 2006, edited by Billy Collins and David Lehman.

"The Ghost-Seer" is excerpted from a verse drama titled *On the Rocks*, portions of which first appeared in different form in *The Cortland Review* and on the website of the Newington-Cropsey Cultural Studies Center (www.nccsc.net). *On the Rocks* was produced as a workshop reading by Richard Ryan and Verse Theater Manhattan, directed by Jim Milton, at the Bowery Poetry Club in New York City on June 16, 2007.

Contents

I

II

For my mother

I

Mother Carey's Hen

There are days I don't think about the sea;
    weeks wash by, in fact,
then a shearwater—or some such—flutters by
on the salt flats fanning out in my mind's eye,
reflected there, a shimmering reverie,
       recalling the pact

I once made (and renew today) to hold
    to a higher altitude.
But note the difference between this bird
and me: a slight disruption or harsh word
and I crash, folded seaward, letting cold
       life intrude;

whereas the petrel, mindless of such height,
    scales each watery hill
that rises up, adapting to the shape
of each impediment, each low escape
instinct in it, the scope of its flight
       fitted to its will.

In the Morning

In the morning, he argued with his wife,
that's how the day began, so he decided
to leave the apartment early, take his time
getting to work. He rode an extra stop
heading downtown and walked up through the park,
bought coffee at the fancy coffee bar,
wanting to treat himself, to ease his mood.

He was first to show up at the office.
Packages were leaning on the jamb.
He keyed the lock and wandered through the door.
Inside, the lights were off; he left them off.
They'd come on soon enough when others came.
At his desk, he scanned his mail, then read an item
on the council member who once shook his hand.

A theater review of a new play
starring a well-known film star caught his eye:
she was stiff and ill-equipped to act on stage,
yet stunningly beautiful, dangerously so,
the critic wrote. He faintly shook his head.
Dangerous, he knew just what that meant.
Out of the dark a voice spilled down the hall,

a rustling, as if somebody were lost.
And then the voice again, deep, almost threatening.
He's not sure why, but for a breath or two
he thought the voice was that of an intruder
and this morning was the last one of his life.

The books on the shelf swam in half focus.
OK, he thought, but the voice did not return.

He thought then of a book he'd read last week,
in which a character takes his own life
by hammering a pair of scissors through
his sternum with the heel of his shoe.
He felt the flesh above his heart and tried
to visualize the passage of the blades.
He looked down at his shoes. The toes were scuffed.

Tonight he will not wander on the way,
or be hit by the bus he's heard about
(the one that cuts down people in their prime).
He's not so young or so naive to think
his death would be that wry or notable.
He'll take the old streets in reverse, the ones
that, traced once more, describe his daily round.

The Call

The call comes and you're out. When you retrieve
the message and return the call, you learn
that someone you knew distantly has died.
His bereaved partner takes you through the news.

She wants to tell you personally how
he fought and, then, how suddenly he went.
She's stunned, and you feel horrible for her,
though somewhat dazed, since he was not a friend,

just someone you saw once or twice a year,
and who, in truth, always produced a shudder:
you confess that you never liked him much,
not to her, of course, but silently to yourself.

You feel ashamed, or rather think the word
ashamed, and hurry off the line. That's when
the image of him appears more vividly,
with nicotine-stained fingertips and hair

like desert weeds fetched up on chicken wire,
the rapacious way he always buttonholed
you at a launch, his breath blowsy with wine.
Well, that will never ever happen again:

one less acquaintance who stops to say hello,
apparently happy at the sight of you.
So why then this surprising queasiness,
not of repulsion but of something like remorse,

that comes on you without your guessing it,
till the thing that nagged you most—his laugh, perhaps—
becomes the very music that you miss,
or think you do, or want to, now he's gone.

Scaffolds

Specter-robed, the ribs of P.S. 1
sway, or seem to sway, under green gauze.
　　Where the restoration's done,
workmen strip the planks and scaffolding
　　　　from spotless brick.

For months (how many now I can't recall),
the building settled into its late age,
　　swaddled in this dingy pall,
till no one could imagine what it looked like
　　　　when it was young

and clean, or even weathered and unclean.
Clean again, at least in part, it shines
　　in midwinter sunlight's gleam
like another kind of ghost, the kind
　　　　that, Lazarus-like,

kicks up his heels to be back in his skin,
or, because skin's hard to inhabit, is glad
　　at least to have survived a season
in that darkened realm the old arrive at, where
　　　　the slate is cleared.

The Good News

A friend calls, so I ask him to stop by.
We sip old Scotch, the good stuff, order in,
some Indian—no frills too fine for him
or me, particularly since it's been
    ages since we made the time.

Two drinks in, we've caught up on our plans.
I've sleepwalked through the last few years by rote;
he's had a nasty rough patch, quote-unquote,
on the home front. So, we commiserate,
    cupping our lowballs in our hands.

It's great to see him, good to have a friend
who feels the same as you about his lot—
that, while some grass is greener, your small plot
is crudely arable, and though you're not
    so young, it's still not quite the end.

As if remembering then, he spills his news.
Though I was pretty lit, I swear it's true,
it was as if a gold glow filled the room
and shone on him, a sun-shaft piercing through
    dense clouds, behind which swept long views.

In that rich light, he looked, not like my friend,
but some acquaintance brushed by on the train.
Had his good fortune kept me from the same,

I had to wonder, a zero-sum game
    that gave the night its early end?

    Nothing strange. Our drinks were done, that's all.
We haven't spoken since. By morning, I
couldn't remember half of what the guy
had said, just his good news, my slurred good-bye,
    the click of the latch, the quiet hall.

The True Mirror

A woman who knows you well has taken you
along a street you've not been down in years,
at dead of winter, to a tenement,
where feral cats quarrel for rancid food,
and leafless trees strain in hard squares of ground.
Though the fact excites you less than as a child,
today's your birthday, this your present, though
your friend has told you nothing of her plan.
She takes your hand, urging you up the last
half-flight of stairs and down a musty hallway
to a door. A small plaque reads MUSEUM OF GLASS.
As she rings the bell, you notice how her hair
lies darkly on her face and think again
of the silent wish you'll never share with her.
A man unlocks the bolt, his voice the same
as the voice that buzzed you in. His room is dark.
At intervals, masked lights illuminate
the motley pieces fused by acetylene
into kaleidoscopic swirls of bottle glass.
On the wall, a wooden box. She now reveals
that this is what she's brought you here to see.
She lifts the velvet curtain, has you lean
and peer inside . . .
                            Consider for a moment
the morning of your earliest memory,
when you came down before your mother did
to find the layer cake she'd made for you
lying in half-light on the kitchen table.
The scene plays in a series of long shots,

the crown of your small head seen from above,
more than thirty years ago.
                              Today, you see
yourself again in this uncanny light,
the way you look to others. But then you blink.
Some phantom in the glass disrupts your gaze,
and you avert your eyes, like an animal
circling sidelong toward its prey.
                              She asks you
what you make of your hidden public self,
your answer good-natured, grateful, and mostly false.
For who was it that stared back in that room?
And who was he to her, whose gift this was?
Too difficult to say, though you might guess
(as she will not), in months and years to come,
at just what this mirror brought to view
before you reeled and turned your face away.

The People

This is the season of dried rushes
and sodden leaf-matter in parks,
when the lightly furred animal bodies
of the people break out in sores

and a mild but insistent contagion
blooms in the chilly dampness.
The lowered sun does not yet warm them,
despite cerulean skies.

The meat-headed race trundles along
in groups, God love them, and their
comforts—blood ties and a stiff Scotch—
suffice somewhat or else not at all.

From a far country comes news
of the current crisis, about which little
is known. Its distant horrors
are rehearsed for a few still listening.

A woman in a shop says, "Maybe
tomorrow," and the eyes of the burghers
streaming across midtown intersections
brighten a moment, then dim.

Others flee on vacation
to a place where they might clear their minds
and hatch a few plans for the future, while
waiting for the weather to improve.

A Brief Scene

It's cheap night at the Whitney. A young man
mills around a large canvas, as a girl
    he's not yet noticed enters in.
He spots her, then begins this small exchange:

his sidelong looks, her turns away, his hands
wringing out his program like a cloth.
    He weighs his least attractive parts—
his sweaty lip, his glasses, his malaise—

against a secret inner quality
that, in his mind, accounts him worthy of her.
    She feels his eyes begin to warm
the skin along one sleeveless arm, her hair

aglow like sunlit water over rocks.
She pauses by the painting on the wall—
    a woman supine in the bath,
her torso flecked with mauve and pale violet—

then walks off, disappeared into the crowd.
Oh, my bitter life, he thinks. There goes
    the one I could be happy with;
she's vanished as if nothing could be simpler.

No creeping thoughts, no remorse, nothing but
a minute's thinning possibility
    unspooling as she let it go,
that is, if she even noticed he was there.

Poor fool, you think, you poor romantic fool,
and leave him there now doubly bereft.
    You've come to see, not pretty girls,
but pictures at a gallery, their women

exquisite, distant, and widely admired,
drawing you with their looks from room to room,
    as unpossessable as light,
and which, once glimpsed, will not leave you alone.

Vigil

Tonight I sit alone
unattended by friends or the sounds
of muted city streets
in August.

Tomorrow our boys will be born,
if science and God's good grace
and my wife's fortitude
hold out

for a little, so that they
will grow, have children or not
have children, also find love
or not,

live long or briefly and fuse
someway into generations,
a future they already bequeath
to us.

It's late. A light flicks on
in the neighbor's bathroom window
and off as he returns
to bed.

The clock blinks on the radiator
and dawn addresses the panes
without brilliance but with a casual
warmth.

Azores

And me,
the temple wall with its votive tablet
shows I have offered my drowned cloak
to the god of the ocean.
Horace, Odes I.5

i

Heeled over on the sea's domed emptiness,
a sail on the horizon slowly yields
its full size, appearing as a shadow, less
a substance than a rumor blown through fields
that the prevailing wind has furrowed white
and black. Now here it is, an hour on.
The sloop has metamorphosed from a kite
drawn on an unseen string, a distant song
the breeze broke up and scattered in our wake,
to a towering spar beneath a charcoal sky,
gaining, massive, on our tiny stern:
an elephant, a senseless lob of strakes,
whose slow approach we patiently discern,
an unintended sharer lying by.

ii

When the last morning lights fade finally—
each foreign sun run roughshod by our own,
which, hoisted up toward noon, looms large, a stone
scattering sparks along a flinty sea—
I am anxious to have them back again,
crowded above the masthead in light wind,
the pole star amber as we crane to find
true north on nights that show no sign of rain.
The memory of them fades in brightened skies,
a secret so refined it cannot brook
the drab unsubtle breeze and public looks
of post meridiem, the way your eyes
spoke candidly to me at first and then
admitted nothing when I looked again.

iii

The vision of a sunset on the ocean:
countless tongues of flame, as if a wood
had roared up just as evening set in motion
its day's-end rituals of neighborhood.
Nearby shelters shudder in the smoke.
In the middle of this fire, there is no reason,
only a vague account of something broken
that we will not miss now—not in this season
of ember-glow and godsent conflagration.
It will be hours on, when the lost light
cools the scene back to sense, that the relation
of what was to what remains will tinge the night
with an acrid fog still clinging in the air
like a manifest of what's no longer there.

iv

If there is one sustaining fact, it's this:
horizon—Manichean anchor of
our darkening half-world, binding the grays above
the main with breaking waves and constant hiss.
Consider for a moment that the line
you gaze along is not the sea and sky,
but sliding forms, a drama for the eye,
a plum disturbance, cello chords, a seine
of drenched debris clogging the world below.

Aloft: a gauzelike exhale and a haze
through which a searchlight sears its blooded rays.
These masses point to nothing we can know.
Perhaps, just this: that it's not possible
to pin the spirit by an act of will.

Hove to: the tiller lashed and set against
a backing foresail trimmed to contradict

a strong impulse to fall off from the wind:
two canceling passions, each one meant to end

the other's outsized wish to turn away
and toward: each countermands the other's sway,

until the bow lies flummoxed in the gale,
stunned and bleating, as the rigging flails

and, heaving, we lie on the cabin floor.
This is what it is to live at war:

sleeplessness, recrimination, shame,
rage, paranoia, cleaving, and the name—

like poison—on my lips no longer the same
one I conjured with before the weather came.

The sky this morning—a scar, whose low sun
          trails breath-shadows over teak,
like Eros flying past on parchment wings
—turns enemy.
          Our natural state is sickness:
(But, as in sickness, did I loathe this food).
What in the weather changes, such that wind,
which needled us to make our way across,
now wants us gone,
          with no trace remaining
of the hull that held us, or the sails
that bellied, as lungs fill, with the very force
of—not love—but aspiration, at least?
Drowned, who could then point to us and say . . .

The eye, at dawn, finds no significance
or object carved into the marble sea
that a pilot could dead reckon from, the lee
as blank as what's to windward. Slow advance,
as stark division swallows its own heels—
the round horizon ends where it begins,
repeatedly, a cyclorama of winds,
a lens trained on high cloud banks that reveals
nothing but blur.
                        Below, the fleshy swells
charge on like herds scenting some distant cue
to move. They crowd together toward a new
safety, harbored and far from warning bells,
till the last rays of the sun recede, then fail,
again without the sighting of a sail.

viii

The sheets and stays go slack in renewed calm,
and, for the first time in a week, our thoughts
race free above this skin of shallow troughs.
Hardly moving waves caress the helm,
as the same stream that urged us on for days
now presses to our sides a guileless hand,
and trade winds peter, free of flux. We stand
unhitching reefs, transfixed by the small ways
sound reasserts itself without the wind:
the gauzy rush of breath, a wheeze of line,
the halyards' endless ticking finally gone
in a warm repose that sunset can't rescind.
We wash ourselves, removing streaks of brine,
new baptized in an hour of halcyon.

ix

A green island draped in volcanic smoke,
imperceptible at first, until the reek
of musk wafts to us seaward over a league,
like the pong of love-sheets a summer night has
     soaked,
retaining, in the after-dawn, the very smell
that brought the madness on. All this we know
before the misted hills float into view.
The fact of land's not what your dreams foretell.
Its bitter law, a wafer on the tongue:
we are not suited to live long at sea.
Though shoreward-days run down as certainly,
they are a habit that we can't unlearn,
like lines creasing the smooth palm of the hand,
this lust for water, fidelity to land.

II

The Visitor

The visitor comes and crowds in at your table.
Where had you met him? Was he with you at school?
You've known him for so many years it's hard
to say exactly when he first appeared.

He helps himself to coffee and a slice
of the Sunday *Times*, his breathing stale with sleep.
His skin gives off the reek of late carousing;
his orange juice, bright as sunlight, hurts your eyes.

Planning for his arrival is no good.
He comes when he comes and always at an hour
you least expect him, sometimes after months
of figuring he's gone once and for all.

He takes his penknife to the morning mail,
looking for an envelope he claims
was sent to him at this address last week.
The visitor becomes accusatory.

He slams the secretary, as your wife
shoos the children into another room.
That's when the painful moment you had hoped
would never be repeated comes again,

snaking through the knotholes in the floor,
unbidden, like the visitor himself,
as she begins to cry—*Who let him in?*
The visit done, her eyes are fixed on you.

333 East 68th Street

On moving day, we mopped the scuffed-out floors,
    amazed at the way the place
had shrunk and how completely dust abhors
a vacuum. Stranded by the doorjamb lay
a tousled broom, a scrap of our old lives.
How had we shoehorned so much of our lives
into four flaking cubes? These rooms had been
our cornucopia and gilded age,
chockablock with babyflesh, a din
that mingled love-cries, clatter, childhood rage.

To see them now, they look so blank, so cheer-
    less that, if it wasn't in
our bones, we'd hardly know we touched ground here,
let alone kept house—first you and then,
when we were married, the two of us, then more:
a skittering dog, a girl, twin boys. With more
bodies than rooms, we made our peace with mess,
close-quartered in chaos, riotously
off-kilter and yet willing to confess
that all our wordless plans had come to be.

Out the bedroom window, through the green
    of the garden, a bell
announces the consecration of the scene
from which we're now outcasts. You say, "Ah, well,
it wouldn't be Eden if we could stay."
But more than anything we wish to stay,
and like Masaccio's Adam, I cast a glance

that syncs with yours, until we look away,
then down, and realize it's not just chance
but our forsaking that makes the memory.

Who bothers to look for what's not lost?
    Some morning, on the bus,
we'll pass this very street marbled in frost
and spin around to catch a glimpse of us
crossing with the children to the park.
But it's early, no one's at the park,
the trees are bare, no couple's walking there.
Craning back we'll see the building fade
like gray exhaust resolving into air
and understand the error that we've made.

My own slipup (the one I made alone)
    was that I came to feel
that happiness had worked into this stone,
into the very brickwork ribbed with steel—
the family seat, a locus, a redoubt
against besieging entropies of doubt,
our castle overlooking feudal land.
But my idolatry of worldly stuff
made a nonsense of the goods at hand,
the precious things I had not loved enough.

Emptied rooms make their own affluence.
    What will last longer than
this stately pile, ivy-wreathed and immense?
The memories of a life-befuddled man
or woman who, in recalling her past,
feels her mother's bathrobe swirling past

or her father's kisses, which she'll soon grow out of.
The architecture of intersecting lives
will find a way to stay, like acts of love,
which not in place but perhaps in time survive.

Yet survive *where*, we wonder, as the day-
    light slants below the panes.
Not here, of course; beyond that we can't say—
on this coast or another, in refrains
at holidays, in other homes than ours,
where if there is still a remnant that is ours,
there will be no occasion for our knowing it.
Dimness: a few last boxes overflow
with things we've tossed aside or kept in going
and arriving in a new place we call home.

The Ghost-Seer

Talent? That's not what they told me in New York.
In fact, I got the definite impression
That quite the opposite was true. I mean
It's not that cool to hole up like Van Gogh
These days and never sell until you're dead.
I don't know. That wasn't even it.
It wasn't that my work didn't appeal—
Not that it did, it definitely did not.
I realized I didn't have the eye.
Well, not the eye exactly. I could draw,
And get a certain look that teachers liked,
But what I lacked was . . . something. Like Cézanne.
That was it, in fact, if you want to know.
Cézanne.

        Let's say Cézanne walks in, his ghost,
Or let's say I could travel back in time,
And I take this picture with me and I show it
To Cézanne. Well, you know, it's not so good.
Seen like that, the painting is absurd.
I mean, Cézanne is why I gave it up.
Because of him. He drove me nuts. It's crazy.
You know, I saw a show of his in Washington,
When I was still in school. Dad took me down.
It was so incredibly typical
Of him. He'd read somewhere about Cézanne,
This major retrospective in D.C.,
And he decided that I had to go.
If I was going to be a painter then
I had to look at art, and he would take me.

It was his way of saying he approved,
Well, not approved, he never really did,
But that he could be big about it all,
He could support his son in his own way,
With the whole thing done of course in the grand style:
Dinner in Georgetown—French—rooms at his club.
But the show, I don't know how best to describe it.
It terrified me. That's the only word.
I found the paintings absolutely terrifying.
The one that stopped me in my tracks was this
Landscape called "The House of the Hanged Man,"
But it wasn't only that one, it was like
One after another of these paintings,
And the thing that I just couldn't figure out
Was how he did it, not just how he made them,
I could see the insane way he handled paint,
With these diagonal strokes that looked like rain,
So that the whole countryside came to life,
Just breathed with this vitality and life,
But it wasn't that. I could aspire to that,
To have good luck and make a picture *move*.
I mean, I'd have to have a lot of luck,
But so you take your chances and maybe then . . .
It's just that I saw in those pictures how
I would never have the merest hint of . . . what?
Of the ability to put my mark on anything,
To reinvent the terms based on the way
I saw the world regardless of the rules.
I didn't have the passion to destroy,
Or if I do, it's totally mundane,
Just your standard viciousness, you know,
Not the kind that you make paintings with, at least.

So I stopped.
                  You know the feeling that I had
The day I quit? I packed up all the paints,
The stretchers and the easels and the tarps,
And I walked them to a dumpster, dropped them in
(This was down on Tenth Street at the time),
And all these kids came by and pulled them out.
Each and every one of them was a painter,
With a studio apartment just like mine,
And fresh paint on their tennis shoes and pants.
So I just handed off the rest and left.
And the feeling as I walked away was not
That I had failed or of the wasted time
I spent imagining that I could paint.
It was a simple feeling, very quiet,
Very contained, of a profound relief.
I felt so totally relieved. And Dad,
Of course, was thrilled. He never said as much.
He knew that if he waited I would quit,
That all he ever had to do was wait,
Though I'm not sure he cared much what I did.
It wasn't like I ever saw him much,
Not only in the City, but anywhere . . .
We never spoke, I hardly ever called him,
He *never* called me, though his secretary did.
And like you said, he never came to Maine.
It wasn't really a big deal, you know.
One year he just stopped coming up.
And that was it, he never came again.
Last week, I thought I saw him on my street.
Can you believe that? Walking on my block.
It's wild. I see him several times a week now.

And it's been going on like this for months.
I started seeing him all over town,
Even before I knew that he was sick,
Which is absolutely nuts and weirder
Even than it sounds because the truth is
He hated New York, never visited.
He always liked his turf or neutral ground.
In the decade that I've lived here, he came once,
For some show I had a painting in downtown,
But he drove home that same night, never saw
My place or met my friends. He hated it,
The City, and I never figured why.
He said the crazy drivers made him nuts,
Which they did, no doubt, but in the end
I always figured it was really me
He didn't want to see, that somehow I
Had turned out like some massive disappointment.
Well, he's the disappointment, as we know.
And every time I saw him I'd lose my breath,
My heart would freak, my legs would both go cold.
And then I'd steel myself, and I'd keep walking
In the direction of my dad, and I'd be smiling
Some nervous plastic smile. Then I'd get close
And I'd think this is nuts, I can't believe
He's here, he never comes here, what the hell?
And then I'd see it wasn't him at all . . .
Just some guy in a polo shirt and glasses.
And I'd feel kind of sick, like all the adrenaline
Had washed up in my stomach. It was never him.
I guess I wonder if I wish it was,
If that's why I keep seeing him like that.
Or maybe that's the way I told myself

That, you know, he was sick and I should give him
Something of a break on account of that.
But, you see, I never knew he was.
No one knew, not even Lionel, and then
It was, like, over. Six months, and he was dead.
So, what is that? You know? I just don't know.
Now, I still see him, like I'm going nuts,
Like my brain has got this solitary thought
That it can't let go.

You want to know the crazy thing? I never
loved him really. And that's what seeing him
Has made me realize. I never did,
At least since I was old enough to know
He didn't really care if I loved him or not.
It was always about the next big business deal.
But I mean what deals? The whole thing's so insane.
There never were big deals, no deals that worked,
As far as I can tell. Last week, we met
With the accountant and there's nothing there.
The trips abroad, the good hotels, the suits,
All Savile Row, were all he cared about.
He always looked the part down to a tee,
But there was nothing underneath it all.
He didn't provide, he was not a provider.
It was all a vast illusion, and now that he's gone
There's nothing left, just lawyers' bills and taxes.
Nothing saved and nothing sheltered, just
The residue of what he lavished on himself.
I never saw him in the hospital.
I couldn't go at first, I was too scared.
And when I finally got there he was unconscious,

Just then, just that hour, almost like he
Knew somehow deep down that I was coming.
So now that he's gone, it's not that I don't miss him.
I can understand he's dead, like mentally,
But I don't feel that sad he's not around.

Befana, a Bedtime Story

In Italy, a woman, we are told,
screwed up her chance to ride to Bethlehem
with the Wise Men for the first Epiphany
(though why they rode that way remains obscure).

Poor gal, she missed her ship, as we'd have done,
or as we *have* done many times before—
despondent on the quay in diesel smoke,
as our liner steams for warmer latitudes.

In Sunday school, when I was young, I learned
that the beggar in the park was Jesus Christ,
as was Aunt Faith who hid her cigarettes
and whose butt-ends were ringed with blood-red Os.

That's just to say He's not so hard to miss:
I still avoid each handout with a wave,
and I never overcame my childish dread
of Aunt Faith's lipstick and nicotine-stale breath.

So here's Befana, who finally figures out
the colossal botch she's made of her long life
(it might have been so different, you see).
She leaves her peasant shack at Christmastime

to stuff strange children's stockings full of sweets.
(Sorry, angel, Daddy didn't mean
to hold so tight. I *like* to give you kisses.)
And so Befana, you know what she does?

She visits little girls while they're in bed,
and leaves them candy in their winter socks,
and that's why now your stocking's hanging up.
Tonight she'll come while you're asleep, and when

she's hidden a new toy or foiled surprise
she'll draw close, as close as I am now,
and in your sleeping face (don't be afraid)
she'll keep watch for the sleeping face of God.

Dog's Life

She has no malice in her.
Her eyes are black love-pools.
The blankness of her mind
cares little for the thought

behind my deeds and misdeeds.
It lights on her needs—for sleep,
for food—as easily as
a moth on a coming leaf.

I am the smarter one,
of course. I judge the world
and the people in it, nudge
my way on a crowded street,

make things happen. She
trails along behind, relies
on me for direction.
She can decide to play

or not to play, her day
a series of win-win choices,
amounting to very little
in the end. A life lived thus:

no fuss, no long regrets,
just the attachment of one
warm being to another
and the ripples that that makes.

I will have a legacy:
some will recall me fondly,
others not. On her, all will
think back with affection,

carry her in their hearts.
For doing what? I ask her.
Not much, she tells me. Nothing?
Not anything at all.

Acceptance Speech

Accept the things you cannot change:
the bleating clock,
the nightly go
—dog leash in tow—
around the block,

neural chemistry,
patchy hair,
a longing stare
and x-ray eye,

and the niggling fact
that things will stay
roughly this way,
to be exact.

Forgive the things you cannot have:
the supple bod,
taut undergrads,
a nicer pad,
long chats with God,

an older name,
your peers' respect,
the oll korrect,
unbridled fame,

a sense of ease
in your own skin,

a lighter burden
by degrees.

The life you'd swap for on the train
(sight unseen)
is much like yours
though it appears
more green.

So, why this pain
that shorts the breath
and spoils your health?
You grow serene—

not yet, but after
your will resigns
a few more times
with heavy laughter.

Lenten Retreat

This year I can't decide
what to do without.
Cigarettes went at New Year's
(they'll be back, no doubt),

but now it's Lent and nothing
occurs to me to undo,
so thinking hard about it,
I'm going to give up you.

No more morning headaches,
no nasty scenes in cabs,
no late nights in restaurants
picking each other's scabs.

After fifteen years (so long!)
of friendship, I've no clue
why we go back for more,
so I'm going to give up you.

In truth, I sort of liked it
—more than liked, in fact—
at least until our opposites
failed to attract.

In time perhaps you'll miss me
and I will miss you too,
but with hardship comes the benefit,
so I will give up you.

Dead Letters

The *A*s are a disaster,
the *B*s are spotty, too,
the *C*s are going faster
than they have a right to do.

Leafing my address book,
I find on every page
countless holes like openwork
(at forty years of age!).

The *D*s and *E*s weren't many,
the *F*s I'll always miss,
the *G*s glow like a penny,
I wanted *H*'s kiss.

Despite the distant *vales*,
I never strike their names—
the *I, J, K*s of Dallas,
the *L*s down on St. James,

the *M*s and *N*s of Upstate,
the *O*s of Waikiki.
P went grimly to her fate,
while *Q* left quietly.

With every letter I broach—
the *R*s on through the *U*s—
my fingers fast approach
the dearest one to lose.

Now even she is gone,
and I, with V, am here,
while W gets X to hum along,
and Z sings in his beer.

Tritina for Susannah

The water off these rocks is green and cold.
The sandless coast takes the tide in its mouth,
as a wolf brings down a deer or lifts its child.

I walked this bay before you were my child.
Your fingers stinging brightly in the cold,
I take each one and warm it in my mouth.

Though I've known this shore for years, my mouth
holds no charms of use to you, my child.
You will have to learn the words to ward off cold

and know them cold, child, in your open mouth.

Very Like a Whale

Having seen the rainstorm letting up,
I step outside and light a cigarette—
a guilty pleasure I allow myself
for now, till guilt (or, horribly, my health)

disallows it as still pleasurable.
A span of windswept gray foregrounds some clouds,
looming presences of various widths.
I play the children's game Prince Hamlet played

and name the shapes parading through the air.
One—it takes me by surprise, in fact—
looks like a woman in the act of love
bent over to accept her lover's loins

in hers, her hair flung backwards as she turns,
urging him on. I thrill and look away.
All hail to nature, for what is this if not
natural, a cause for giving thanks?

Another drag, and when I look again,
only an instant later, it is gone.
The shape betrays no shade of what it was,
changed from anything my game can guess,

a force without a form, a welling fog
stripped of its human lines and featureless,
dark, opaque, a brooding leviathan
breaching as the rain begins again.